Freezer Meal Prep
A 35 Day Menu Plan

By

Ann L. Koretz

Thank you to Katrina Gentry and Kenneth Gentry for believing in and encouraging me. And a special thanx to Kenneth for walking through the publishing process.

Annie's House Publishing

www.annieshousepublishing.com

Copyright © 2018 Ann Koretz

All rights reserved.

ISBN: 1717583954
ISBN-13: 978-1717583956

Why Would You Prepare Meals in Bulk?

When you prepare 35 or more meals at one time you save **money** and **time**! You can save money by buying foods in bulk, or stocking up when things are on sale. You'll save time preparing all the meals at once, plus you'll save time every night making the meals.

You can save time by using freezer bags. Mix everything in the bag and you have less dishes to wash.

You don't have to make all 35 meals at one time - you can break it down to 7 or 14 meals at a time.

This note is divided into 5 weeks, each with 7 meals. Each week's menu consists of: 1 ground meat recipe, 1 fish recipe, 1 pork meal, 2 chicken, and 2 beef meals. If you don't eat beef or fish, most recipes can be adapted to other proteins like chicken.

Each week has a grocery list for all 7 meals and a mini grocery list for each meal. At the end there is a grocery list for all 35 meals if you want to do one month at a time.

And, of course, you can double these recipes and make twice as many!

When cooking in bulk, you can prepare several bags of cooked ground beef or turkey to use for easy pasta meals, sloppy Joe's or tacos.

All of the meals in this booklet are designed to feed four people. The meals are for the main course; in some cases you should prepare a side dish or salad with it.

As you go through these recipes, remember, **you** are the cook! You can add more of something, less of something or leave something out! Do it to your taste.

Also, if a recipe calls for something like a pork butt roast, but pork shoulders are on sale, get that!

Foods That Do Not Freeze Well

- Fried foods
- Fruits and veggies with high water content (cucumber, melon, cabbage and lettuce)
- Mayo
- Whipping cream
- Yogurt
- Raw potatoes (unless there is liquid in the recipe)
- Mushrooms (unless there is liquid in the recipe)
- Sour cream

What You Will Need

You want to save as much time as possible, so here are some things you can use to streamline your prep time:

✱ Gallon sized freezer bags (you will need at least one for each meal). Some meals will need two bags. Always have a few extra in case of leaks. Using freezer bags to prepare meals also saves time in washing bowls and spoons.

✱ A marker to mark the freezer bags with.

✱ Recipes!

✱ Something to hold the bags upright while you fill them. I use containers that I found at a dollar store.

✱ At least two sets of measuring cups.

✱ At least two sets of measuring spoons.

✱ A small grater (or two).

✱ Sharp knives and a cutting board.

✱ Can opener.

✱ A juicer.

✱ An apron.

✱ A nearby trash can.

✱ A can drainer. You can use this for catching seeds in citrus that you squeeze too.

✱ Paper towels.

✱ One or two spoons.

✱ Food processor or chopper.

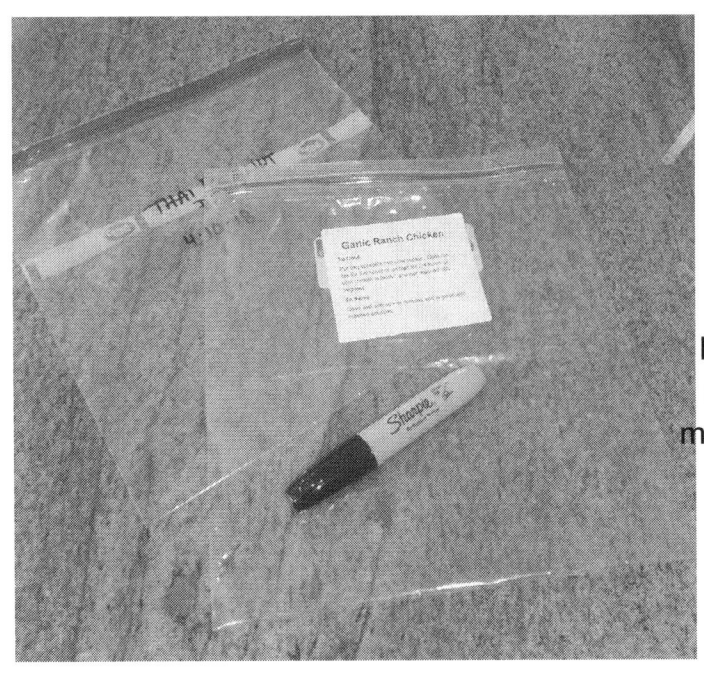

Label your freezer bags (or other containers) with the name of the meal, the date and, if you want, add cooking instructions.

You'll need something to hold your bags up and open. This will also keep the zipper part of the bag clean. Check dollar stores.

Tips for Bulk Meal Prep -

When preparing meals to freeze add all ingredients except meat. Seal the bag and mix. Add meat and mix again. Then squeeze all the air out and seal tightly. Any air in the bag could create freezer burn.

Make sure you are using *freezer* bags, not storage bags.

If you have a drawer in your freezer, freeze the bags flat. Once frozen, you can stand them in the drawer. Then you can flip through them like a file.

You can freeze all like-meats on one freezer shelf, or put them in alphabetically, or put one week's worth of meals together. Whatever makes more sense to you.

Label the bags with the meal name and the date. You can also save time by listing how to prepare the meal.

Spend a little extra and get a jar of crushed garlic! It will save you a lot of time and work.

Use slow cooker liners to save clean up time.

Do it with a friend! Buy double of everything, then put together two of each meal and split them.

Don't try to do everything in one day, split it up -

Day one, plan your meals and shopping list. Label (with a marker) all of your freezer bags. Recipe ~ Date ~ How to cook.

Day two, do all of your grocery shopping.

Day three, put all the meals together and freeze.

Important - *never* defrost bags on the counter! Always defrost them in the fridge overnight. Then you can pop the contents into the slow cooker in the morning or cook them quickly (on the grill, stovetop, pressure cooker or oven) in the evening.

Get into a rhythm - in the morning take a dinner for tomorrow out of the freezer and put it into the fridge to defrost. Take the defrosted meal bag from the fridge and put into the slow cooker.

Handy Measurements to Have

Onions -

Small onion = 4 ounces by weight or about ½ cup chopped.
Medium onion = 8 ounces, or about 1 cup chopped.
Large onion = 12 ounces, or about 1½ cups chopped.
Jumbo onion = 16 ounces, or about 2 cups chopped.

Crushed garlic -

1 teaspoon of crushed garlic = 1 clove of fresh garlic

Splitting Ingredients in Half

Recipe Calls for:	In Half:
3/4 cup	6 tablespoons
2/3 cup	1/3 cup
1/2 cup	1/4 cup
1/3 cup	2 tbsp + 2 tsp
1/4 cup	2 tablespoons
1 tablespoon	1.5 teaspoons
1 teaspoon	1/2 teaspoon
1/2 teaspoon	1/4 teaspoon

Freezer Meal FAQs

Q - Can I use frozen ingredients to make the freezer meals?

A - If you have frozen meats, veggies or other ingredients, keep them frozen, don't defrost them to put them in the meal and then refreeze.

Q - How many servings do these recipes make?

A - All of the recipes in this booklet make 4 adult servings. You can double them to make them for 8 (put in two freezer bags). If you need 6 servings use the table on the previous page to halve the recipes then use one and a half times the amounts quoted.

Q - How long do the meals last in the freezer?

A - If your freezer is set at 0 degrees or less, the meals should last at least 3 to 6 months.

Q - How long will the meal last in the refrigerator after it is defrosted if I don't cook it right away?

A - If you defrost a meal in your fridge and don't use it right away, you should cook it within 3 days. If you won't be able to eat it right away, cook the meal and then refreeze it.

Q - Can I defrost the meals in the microwave?

A - Microwaves tend to defrost unevenly and toughen some of the ingredients.

Q - Can I put these meals into the slow cooker frozen?

A - Because parts of the meal will thaw and cook at different rates it's not suggested to cook them from frozen.

Q - Is there a quick way to defrost these meals if I forget to take them out of the freezer?

A - Depending on the meal, some can be run under warm water for a few minutes to help them defrost.

Q - What can I do if the meal is completely frozen and I need to cook it?

A - If you must cook a meal from frozen, break it into pieces, if possible, then put it in your slow cooker on low. Stir every few minutes. Once it is mostly defrosted, start the cooking time.

Q - How often should I stir these meals while they are cooking in the slow cooker?

A - Every time you open the slow cooker, you will need to add about 5 minutes of cooking time. Only open the cooker if the recipe calls for the meal to be stirred.

Q - Do I have to use the exact ingredients called for in the recipes?

A - NO! Adjust them to your taste! If a similar meat used in a recipe is on sale, use that! If you don't like spicy food, don't use hot spices. But if you take out a spice, replace it with something - either more pepper or a less "spicy" spice like garlic or ginger.

Q - Can I use less salt? If I do, will the food be bland?

A - Add flavor to recipes by adding citrus zest, garlic or ginger.

Q - What is QR and NR?

A - For pressure cookers - **QR** is Quick Release / **NR** is Natural Release.

Stock Up and Freeze

Something quick to do is use freezer bags to marinate meat. If there is a sale on something, grab a bunch. Put them into individual freezer bags with various marinades. Then you can grab them to build a meal around.

Here are some ideas to put away to grill later or put in your slow cooker -

Chicken Pieces -

Put your chicken in a freezer bag, add some olive oil and any of the following -

- Lemon & Dill
- Italian Seasoning
- Lime & Cilantro
- Balsamic Vinegar
- Garlic & Onion
- Rosemary Leaves
- Lemon & Pepper
- Teriyaki Sauce
- Crushed Pineapple
- Bar-B-Q sauce (no oil needed)

Beef (Steak or Roast) -

Marinating meat helps to make it more tender. For beef try -

- Dijon Mustard
- Balsamic Vinegar
- Olive Oil & Minced Garlic
- Teriyaki Sauce
- Any Meat Rub
- Lemon & Garlic
- Cola Soft Drink
- Papaya Skins (to tenderize)
- Fresh Grated Ginger

Pork Chops -

- Soy Sauce & Lemon
- Brown Sugar & Spicy Mustard
- Balsamic Vinegar
- Olive Oil & Italian Spice Blend
- Worcestershire sauce
- Onion Powder & Sliced Onions

Things to Do With Cooked Meat

Whether it's ground beef, turkey, chicken or pork, you can cook a big batch and split it up into one pound bags, freeze and use later.

Cook the meat alone, with chopped onions, bell peppers and/or garlic. Add taco seasoning, Italian seasoning, chipotle spice or bar-b-q sauce.

Later, defrost one to make -

- Mix with gravy and serve over pasta or rice
- Spaghetti or pasta sauce
- Sloppy Joes
- Tacos
- Burritos
- Taco salad
- Nachos
- Add it to a soup
- Top a pizza

You can also cook whole chickens and pull the meat off. Use it for -

- Mix with a jar of gravy and serve over pasta or rice
- Warm with a can of cream of chicken or mushroom soup and add to cooked pasta
- White chili
- Salad
- Burritos
- Tacos
- Enchiladas
- Add it to a soup
- Quesadillas

Slow Cooking Conversion Times

The meals in this book were developed to be cooked in a slow cooker. I have converted the recipes to be cooked in a pressure cooker (Instant Pot) also. But if you would rather cook them in the oven or stovetop, you can. Below is a chart to help you if you plan to cook them in an oven.

Low cooking time	High cooking time	Oven or stovetop cooking time
4 to 6 hours	1.5 to 2.5 hours	15 to 30 minutes
6 to 8 hours	3 to 4 hours	35 to 40 minutes
8 to 10 hours	6 to 8 hours	50 minutes to 3 hours

Pressure Cooker General Cooking Times

The new electric pressure cookers (instant pots) are great! Especially if you planned to put your dinner in the slow cooker, but forgot! They cook faster but still serve up tender meats.

Always remember that you need about 1 cup of liquid in your cooker in order for it to build up pressure.

I've listed cooking instructions on most of the recipes for pressure cookers. But here is a general guide -

Chicken breasts	6 to 8 minutes	QR
Cubed chicken	6 minutes	OR
Beef roasts	20 to 25 minutes	QR
Cubed beef	20 minutes	QR
Pork chops	15 minutes	QR
Pork roasts	15 minutes	QR
Fish/Seafood	Whole - 5 minutes Fillet - 3 minutes	QR

Menu #1

Balsamic Beef Roast with Carrots

Carne Asada

Raspberry Chipotle Chicken

Ginger Peach Chicken

Swedish Meatballs

Ranch Pork Chops

Teriyaki Shrimp

Menu #1 Grocery List

Meats
2 pound boneless beef chuck shoulder roast
1 (2 pound) flank steak
4 servings of chicken pieces (with or without bones)
2 pounds boneless, skinless chicken breasts
1 pound large shrimp, peeled and deveined
4 thick sliced boneless pork chops

Produce
5 carrots
1 orange
2 limes
1 cup fresh cilantro
1 jalapeno
1 red onion
1 small brown onion
1 cup fresh mushrooms
6 to 8 medium potatoes
1 pound broccoli florets
3 tablespoons grated ginger

Packaged
3 tablespoons rice vinegar
1/2 cup balsamic vinegar
1 tablespoon soy sauce
3/4 cup honey
1 cup raspberry syrup or preserves
3 tablespoons brown sugar
8 tablespoons soy sauce
1/2 cup olive oil
2 packages dry Ranch Dressing mix
1 teaspoon cornstarch
1 (10¾ ounce) can cream of mushroom soup
2 cans cream of chicken soup
2 cups beef broth
½ cup orange juice
jar of crushed garlic (6 tablespoons)

Frozen
1 (28 ounce) bag frozen meatballs
16 ounce bag frozen peach slices

Dairy
1 cup milk

Spices
1 tablespoon chipotle seasoning
1/4 teaspoon red pepper flakes
1 tablespoon dill
½ teaspoon paprika
salt & pepper

Things to Prep for Menu #1

Cut carrots into bite size pieces

Slice red onion

Chop mushrooms

Cut potatoes into large pieces

Cut 4 chicken breasts into strips

Balsamic Beef Roast with Carrots

INGREDIENTS:

2 pounds boneless beef chuck shoulder roast

5 carrots, peeled and cut into bite-sized pieces

1/2 cup honey

1/2 cup balsamic vinegar

1 tablespoon soy sauce

1 teaspoon salt

1/4 teaspoon red pepper flakes

3 tablespoons crushed garlic

Zest of 1/2 an orange

To Prepare:

Place all items in freezer bag. Let air out and seal. Freeze until ready to use.

To Cook:

Defrost in fridge overnight.

SLOW COOKER - Place bag contents in slow cooker and cook on low for 8 to 12 hours or until beef shreds easily and carrots are soft. If it starts to dry out, add a little water, balsamic vinegar or beef broth.

PRESSURE COOKER - Place bag contents in slow cooker and cook on high for 25 minutes. NR for 5 minutes.

Shred beef and serve.

To Serve: Serve with a salad.

Note: You can also add small white potatoes before cooking.

Carne Asada

INGREDIENTS:
2 limes, juiced
1 tablespoon crushed garlic
½ cup orange juice
1 cup chopped fresh cilantro
½ teaspoon salt
¼ teaspoon black pepper
¼ cup olive oil
1 jalapeno, minced
2 tablespoons white vinegar
1 (2 pound) flank steak

To prepare:

Place all ingredients except meat into a large freezer bag. Squeeze it around to mix it up. Put the entire steak into the bag. Seal it up tight. Make sure all the meat is exposed to the marinade, squishing the bag around to coat. Let air out and seal. Freeze until ready to use.

To cook:

Defrost in fridge overnight.

Heat an outdoor grill to high heat.

Remove the flank steak from the marinade, and discard excess marinade. Cook on the grill for 7 to 10 minutes per side.

Once done, remove from heat and let rest 10 minutes. Slice against the grain, and serve.

Raspberry Chipotle Chicken

INGREDIENTS:

4 servings of chicken pieces
1 cup raspberry syrup or preserves
1 tablespoon chipotle seasoning

To Prepare:

Place all items in freezer bag. Let air out and seal. Freeze until ready to use.

To Cook:

Defrost in fridge overnight.

SLOW COOKER - Place bag contents in slow cooker. Cook on high 6 to 7 hours.

PRESSURE COOKER - Place bag contents in pressure cooker with ½ cup water. Cook for 7 minutes on high. NR for 5 minutes.

Ginger Peach Chicken

INGREDIENTS:

4 boneless, skinless chicken breasts
16 ounce bag frozen peach slices
1 sliced red onion
3 tablespoons brown sugar
3 tablespoons soy sauce
2 tablespoons grated ginger
1/2 teaspoon black pepper

To Prepare:

Cut chicken into strips. Place all items in freezer bag. Let air out and seal. Freeze until ready to use.

To Cook:

Defrost bag in fridge before cooking.

SLOW COOKER -
Place bag contents in slow cooker and cook on low for 8 to 9 hours.

PRESSURE COOKER - Place bag contents in pressure cooker and cook on high for 6 minutes. NR for 5 minutes.

To Serve:

Serve over rice with a salad or veggie.

Swedish Meatballs

INGREDIENTS:

1 (28 ounce) bag frozen meatballs
1 (10¾ ounce) can cream of mushroom soup
2 cups beef broth
1 cup fresh mushrooms, chopped
½ cup diced onion
1 tablespoon dill
½ teaspoon paprika
½ teaspoon salt
½ teaspoon pepper

DAY OF -

1 cup sour cream

To Prepare:

Place all ingredients except for the sour cream into a freezer bag. Mix well, let air out and seal. Freeze until ready to use.

To Cook:

Thaw overnight in refrigerator before cooking.

SLOW COOKER - Place bag contents in slow cooker. Cook on high for 4-6 hours or low for 8-10. Mix in sour cream the last 30 minutes of cooking.

PRESSURE COOKER - Place bag contents in slow cooker with ½ cup water. Cook on high for 5 minutes on high. QR. Mix in sour cream the last 30 minutes of cooking.

To Serve:

This is great served over noodles. You can also serve them on rice.

Creamy Ranch Pork Chops and Potatoes

INGREDIENTS:

4 thick sliced boneless pork chops
6 to 8 medium potatoes, chopped into large pieces
2 cans cream of chicken soup
2 packages dry Ranch Dressing mix
1 cup milk

To Prepare:

Put all ingredients except chops in a freezer bag. Mix well and add chops. Let air out and seal. Freeze until ready to use.

To Cook:

Thaw overnight in refrigerator before cooking.

SLOW COOKER - Place bag contents in slow cooker and cook on high for 3 to 4 hours or low for 6 to 7 hours.

PRESSURE COOKER - Place bag contents in pressure cooker and cook on high for 5 minutes. NR for 5 minutes.

To Serve:

Use the sauce in the cooker as gravy for the potatoes and the pork chops.

Teriyaki Shrimp

INGREDIENTS:

1 pound large shrimp, peeled and deveined with tails removed
1 pound broccoli florets
1 tablespoon olive
5 tablespoons soy sauce
1 tablespoon rice vinegar
1 tablespoon honey
2 tablespoons crushed garlic
1 tablespoon fresh grated ginger
1 teaspoon cornstarch

DAY OF -
1 package angel hair pasta
Green onions, sliced
1 tablespoon sesame seeds

To prepare:
Combine all ingredients in freezer bag and mix well. Freeze until ready to use.

To cook:
Defrost in fridge overnight.

This meal can be made in a slow cooker or in a skillet on the stove.

SLOW COOKER - place bag contents into slow cooker and cook on low for 4 to 5 hours.

SKILLET - place bag contents into large skillet on medium heat. Cook for about 5 to 6 minutes (until shrimp has turned pink).

Cook pasta and add to slow cooker or skillet. Toss well.

To serve sprinkle with green onions and sesame seeds.

Menu #1 Meal Grocery Lists

Balsamic Beef Roast with Carrots
2 pounds boneless beef chuck shoulder roast
5 carrots, peeled and cut into bite-sized pieces
1/2 cup honey
1/2 cup balsamic vinegar
1 tablespoon soy sauce
1 teaspoon salt
1/4 teaspoon red pepper flakes
3 tablespoons crushed garlic
Zest of 1/2 an orange

Swedish Meatballs
1 (28 ounce) bag frozen meatballs
1 (10¾ ounce) can cream of mushroom soup
2 cups beef broth
1 cup fresh mushrooms, chopped
½ cup diced onion
1 tablespoon dill
½ teaspoon paprika
½ teaspoon salt
½ teaspoon pepper

Teriyaki Shrimp
1 pound large shrimp, peeled and deveined
1 pound broccoli florets
1 tablespoon olive
5 tablespoons soy sauce
1 tablespoon rice vinegar
1 tablespoon honey
2 tablespoons crushed garlic
1 tablespoon fresh grated ginger
1 teaspoon cornstarch

Carne Asada
2 limes, juiced
1 tablespoon crushed garlic
½ cup orange juice
1 cup chopped fresh cilantro
½ teaspoon salt
¼ teaspoon black pepper
¼ cup olive oil
1 jalapeno, minced
2 tablespoons white vinegar
1 (2 pound) flank steak

Ginger Peach Chicken
2 pounds boneless, skinless chicken breasts
16 ounce bag frozen peach slices
1 sliced red onion
3 tablespoons brown sugar
3 tablespoons soy sauce
2 tablespoons grated ginger
1/2 teaspoon black pepper

Raspberry Chipotle Chicken
4 servings of chicken pieces
1 cup raspberry syrup or preserves
1 tablespoon chipotle seasoning

Ranch Pork Chops
4 thick sliced boneless pork chops
6 to 8 medium potatoes, chopped into large pieces
2 cans cream of chicken soup
2 packages dry Ranch Dressing mix
1 cup milk

Menu #2

Beef & Broccoli
BBQ Beef Ribs
Honey Sesame Chicken
French Chicken

Taco Soup
Apple Cherry Pork Loin
Marinated Fish

Menu #2 Grocery List

Meats

4 fresh tuna, salmon or swordfish filets

2 pound boneless pork loin

1 pound lean ground beef

8 chicken breasts

2 to 3 pounds boneless beef ribs

2 pounds steak (flank is ideal but any works)

Produce

2 large onions, cut into wedges

1 small onion

1 apple

1 stalk of celery

1 teaspoon fresh ginger

Packaged

1 can beef broth

1 can of whole berry cranberry sauce

1 can diced tomatoes

1 can red kidney beans

1 can black beans

1 can whole kernel corn

1 cup ketchup

1 small bottle bar-b-q sauce

1/2 cup Worcestershire sauce

2 cups orange juice

¾ cups apple juice

3 tablespoons lemon juice

8 ounce bottle of French dressing

1 packet of dry onion soup mix

3 cups soy sauce

¼ cup olive oil

5 tablespoons sesame oil

1/3 cup brown sugar

1 cup honey

4 tablespoon sesame seeds

1 jar of crushed garlic (4 teaspoons)

Frozen

1 cup pitted cherries

Spices

Ground coriander

Chipotle seasoning

Fresh or dried dill

Cumin

Paprika

Chili powder

Onion powder

salt & pepper

Things to Prep for Menu #2

Cut 2 onions into wedges

Cut steak into thin slices

Cut ribs apart, if needed

Cut chicken breasts into strips, if desired

Cook ground beef and cool

Beef and Broccoli

INGREDIENTS:
2 pounds thinly sliced beef (flank is ideal but any works)
1 can beef broth
1/2 cup soy sauce
1/3 cup brown sugar
2 teaspoons minced garlic
1 tablespoon lemon juice
1 teaspoon ground coriander
1 teaspoon fresh ginger
1 tablespoon Sesame oil
DAY OF –
2 tablespoon Cornstarch
1 package frozen broccoli or 1 pound fresh

To Prepare:
Put all ingredients except cornstarch and broccoli in a zip lock freezer bag. Mix well. Freeze until ready to use.

To Cook:
Thaw overnight in refrigerator before cooking.

SLOW COOKER -
Put bag contents into slow cooker on low for 5-6 hours. Remove 1/4 cup of sauce mix well with corn starch then stir back into crock pot.
Add Broccoli, stir and cook 30 more minutes.

PRESSURE COOKER - This meal turns out much better in a slow cooker.

To Serve:
Serve over cooked rice or noodles. Add a salad or veggie on the side.

Baked BBQ Beef Ribs

2 to 3 pounds boneless beef ribs

1 cup ketchup

1 small bottle bar-b-q sauce

1/2 cup Worcestershire sauce

1 Tablespoon onion powder

2 large onions, cut into wedges

To Prepare:

If needed, cut ribs apart. Combine everything in a freezer bag.   Mix well. Seal bag and freeze.

To Cook:

Thaw overnight in refrigerator before cooking.

This meal turns out *best* in the oven.

OVEN - I like these the best when done in the oven! Put in baking dish and add about 1 inch of water. Cover with foil and bake at 350 degrees for about 2 hours. Take foil off about 15 minutes before done.

SLOW COOKER - Place mixture in slow cooker and add 1/2 cup water. Cook on low for 5 to 6 hours or until cooked through and tender. Check every couple of hours and add about 1/4 cup water if it starts drying out.

PRESSURE COOKER - Place mixture in pressure cooker and add 1/4 cup water. Cook for 20 minutes. QR.

To Serve:

Goes well served over rice or mashed potatoes. Good with most any veggie.

Honey Sesame Chicken

Ingredients

4 chicken breasts
¼ cup olive oil
1 cup honey
½ cup soy sauce
4 tablespoons sesame oil
2 tablespoons lemon juice
1 teaspoon crushed garlic
4 tablespoon sesame seeds
Salt & pepper to taste

To Prepare:

Cut chicken into strips. Put all items except chicken into freezer bag. Mix well. Add chicken to the bag. Mix again.

Remove air, seal and freeze until ready for use.

To Cook:

Defrost bag in fridge before cooking.

Oven - Place contents in baking dish. Bake at 325° for one hour. This way will make the skin crispy if you leave it on.

SLOW COOKER - Cook on low for 4 to 5 hours.

PRESSURE COOKER - Cook for 6 minutes. QR.

To Serve: Serve with any veggie or salad. Great over rice. You can sprinkle with toasted sesame seeds if desired.

French Chicken

INGREDIENTS:

4 chicken breasts

1 can of whole berry cranberry sauce

8 ounce bottle of French dressing

1 packet of dry onion soup mix

To Prepare:

Cut chicken into strips. Place all items except chicken in freezer bag. Smash ingredients together to combine. Add chicken. Let air out and seal. Freeze until ready to use.

To Cook:

Defrost in fridge overnight.

SLOW COOKER -

Place bag contents in slow cooker and cook on low for 4 to 6 hours.

PRESSURE COOKER - Cook for 7 minutes. QR.

Taco Soup

INGREDIENTS:

1 pound lean ground beef
1 can diced tomatoes
1 can red kidney beans
1 can black beans
1 can whole kernel corn
1 tablespoon Chipotle
   seasoning
1 tablespoon fresh or dried dill
1/2 teaspoon cumin
1/2 teaspoon paprika

1/2 teaspoon chili powder
1 teaspoon crushed garlic
1/2 teaspoon onion powder
Pinch of salt

DAY OF -
Grated Cheddar Cheese
Sour Cream
Tortilla chips
Lemon or lime wedges

To Prepare:

Brown ground beef until cooked through, let cool. Place cooled beef in freezer bag and add all other ingredients (drain the corn but not the other items). Mix well. Freeze until ready to use.

To Cook:

Thaw overnight in refrigerator before cooking.

SLOW COOKER - Cook for 3 to 4 hours on high or 6 to 8 hours on low.

PRESSURE COOKER - Cook for 1 minute! QR or NR and keep warm.

For a "soupier" soup - add a can of beef broth when cooking.

To Serve:

Serve with a dollop of sour cream and grated cheddar cheese. Tortilla chips make a great "spoon" for this chunky soup.

Apple Cherry Pork Loin

INGREDIENTS:

2 pound boneless pork loin
1 cup diced apple
¾ cups apple juice
½ cups water
1 cup pitted cherries
½ cups diced onion
½ cups diced celery
⅛ teaspoon salt
⅛ teaspoon black pepper

To Prepare:

Combine all ingredients except pork in a freezer bag. Mix well. Add pork, Let air out and seal. Freeze until ready to use.

To Cook:

Defrost bag in fridge before cooking.

SLOW COOKER - Place bag contents into a slow cooker. Cook on high for 4 to 5 hours or until pork is cooked through.

PRESSURE COOKER - Place bag contents into a pressure cooker. Cook on high for 15 minutes. QR.

To Serve:

Serve with potatoes and a veggie.

Marinated Fish Fillets

INGREDIENTS:

4 tuna, salmon or swordfish filets (fresh not frozen)

2 cups soy sauce

2 cups orange juice

To Prepare:

Place all items into a freezer bag. Mix carefully. Freeze.

To Cook:

Thaw overnight in refrigerator before cooking.

These are best grilled on the bar-b-q, but they can also be grilled or baked in the oven. They only take about 10 minutes on each side. If you put them in the oven, add a little of the marinade in the baking dish. On the bar-b-q, just discard the marinade.

To Serve:

Yummy with a fruit salad and green beans or cooked carrots.

Menu #2 Meal Grocery Lists

Beef & Broccoli
2 pounds thinly sliced beef (flank is ideal but any works)
1 can beef broth
1/2 cup soy sauce
1/3 cup brown sugar
1-2 cloves minced garlic
1 tablespoon lemon juice
1 teaspoon ground coriander
1 teaspoon fresh ginger
1 Tablespoon Sesame oil

Honey Sesame Chicken
4 chicken breasts
¼ cup olive oil
1 cup honey
½ cup soy sauce
4 tablespoons sesame oil
2 tablespoons lemon juice
1 teaspoon crushed garlic
4 tablespoon sesame seeds
Salt & pepper to taste

Taco Soup
1 pound lean ground beef
1 can diced tomatoes
1 can red kidney beans
1 can black beans
1 can whole kernel corn
1 tablespoon Chipotle seasoning
1 tablespoon fresh or dried dill
1/2 teaspoon cumin
1/2 teaspoon paprika
1/2 teaspoon chili powder
1 teaspoon crushed garlic
1/2 teaspoon onion powder
Pinch of salt

BBQ Beef Ribs
2 to 3 pounds boneless beef ribs
1 cup ketchup
1 small bottle bar-b-q sauce
1/2 cup Worcestershire sauce
1 Tablespoon onion powder
2 large onions, cut into wedges

French Chicken
4 chicken breasts
1 can of whole berry cranberry sauce
8 ounce bottle of French dressing
1 packet of dry onion soup mix

Apple Cherry Pork Loin
2 pound boneless pork loin
1 cup diced apple
¾ cups apple juice
½ cups water
1 cup pitted cherries
½ cups diced onion
½ cups diced celery
⅛ teaspoon salt
⅛ teaspoon black pepper

Marinated Fish
4 tuna, salmon or swordfish filets (fresh not frozen)
2 cups soy sauce
2 cups orange juice

Menu #3

Mongolian Beef
Salsa Beef
Sri Lankan Coconut Chicken
Creamy Italian Chicken

Cowboy Casserole
Luau Pork (Kalua Pig)
Orange Shrimp

Menu #3 Grocery List

Meats

1.5 pounds flank steak
1.5 pounds beef stew meat
4 boneless chicken breasts
4 chicken breasts
1 pound ground beef
A 4 to 5 pound pork butt roast or pork shoulder roast

Produce

2 small onions
1.5 cups shredded carrots
2 lemons
1 orange
1 lime
2 tablespoons fresh ginger

Packaged

1 small can sliced olives
1 can whole corn
1 can red kidney beans
1 can stewed tomatoes
1 can of cream of chicken soup
3/4 cup soy sauce
3 tablespoons liquid smoke flavoring

3/4 cup honey
About 1 cup olive oil
2 cups salsa
1 can coconut milk or cream (not water)
At least 6 tablespoons crushed garlic
1/2 cup shredded (unsweetened) coconut
1 small bottle of Italian dressing
1/4 cup orange juice

Frozen

1 pound fresh cooked shrimp, cleaned
1 bag frozen broccoli

Dairy

8 ounce package of cream cheese

Spices

Cinnamon
Ground turmeric
Fresh fennel, minced or fennel seed, crushed
1 teaspoon Italian seasoning
Chili powder or chipotle spice blend
Crushed red pepper flakes
Salt & pepper

Things to Prep for Menu #3

Cut chicken breasts in half lengthwise (like strips)

Cook ground beef with 1 chopped onion

Mongolian Beef

INGREDIENTS:

1-1/2 pounds flank steak, cut into strips

2 tablespoons olive oil

1 teaspoon grated fresh ginger

3/4 cup soy sauce

3/4 cup honey

1/2 cup water

1 cup shredded carrots

1/2 brown onion, chopped

Juice of one lemon

2 tablespoons minced garlic

To Prepare:

Put all ingredients in a freezer bag. Mix well. Freeze until ready to use.

To Cook:

Thaw overnight in refrigerator before cooking

SLOW COOKER - . Put bag contents into slow cooker. Cook on low for 6-8 hours.

PRESSURE COOKER - Put bag contents into pressure cooker. Cook on high for 18 minutes. QR.

To Serve:

Serve over cooked rice. Add a salad or veggie on the side.

Salsa Beef

INGREDIENTS:

1.5 pounds beef stew meat

2 cups salsa

1 tablespoon crushed garlic

2 tablespoons lemon juice

To Prepare:

Place all items in freezer bag. Mix well. Let air out and seal. Freeze until ready to use.

To Cook:

Defrost in fridge overnight.

SLOW COOKER - Place bag contents in slow cooker. Cook on low for 8 to 10 hours.

PRESSURE COOKER - Place bag contents in pressure cooker. Cook on low for 18 minutes. NR for 5 minutes then QR.

To Serve:

Serve over rice or as tacos or burritos.

Sri Lankan Coconut Chicken

INGREDIENTS:

4 boneless chicken breasts
1 can coconut milk or cream (not water)
1 teaspoon crushed garlic
¼ onion, minced
1 teaspoon ground turmeric
1 teaspoon fresh fennel, minced or 1 teaspoon fennel seed, crushed
1 tablespoon fresh ginger, grated
Black pepper to taste
Juice from 1 lime
A pinch of chili flakes (if desired)
Salt to taste
½ teaspoon cinnamon
1/2 cup shredded (unsweetened) coconut

DAY OF - more shredded (unsweetened) coconut

To Prepare:

Place 1 cup coconut in a freezer bag. Pound the coconut to grind it smaller. Add all other ingredients except chicken. Mix well. Cut chicken breasts in half lengthwise. Put into freezer bag. Let air out and seal. Freeze until ready to use.

To Cook:

Defrost bag in fridge before cooking.

SLOW COOKER - Place bag contents in slow cooker. Cook on high for 5 to 6 hours.

PRESSURE COOKER - Place bag contents in pressure cooker. Cook on high for 6 minutes. QR.

To Serve:

Before serving, sprinkle with additional shredded coconut. Serve over rice with a salad or veggie.

Note:

You can also add 1 to 2 teaspoons curry powder to the ingredients for a coconut curry chicken.

Creamy Italian Chicken

INGREDIENTS:

4 chicken breasts, cut into strips if desired

8 ounce package of cream cheese

1 can of cream of chicken soup

1 small bottle of Italian dressing

1 teaspoon Italian seasoning

To Prepare:

Soften cream cheese and place in freezer bag with cream of chicken soup, Italian dressing and seasoning. Mix well. Add chicken. Let air out and seal. Freeze until ready to use.

To Cook:

Thaw overnight in refrigerator before cooking.

SLOW COOKER - Place bag contents in slow cooker. Cook on Low for 4-6 hours.

PRESSURE COOKER - Place bag contents in pressure cooker. Cook on high for 7 minutes. QR

To Serve:

Serve a salad and veggie of your choice.

Cowboy Casserole

INGREDIENTS:

1 pound ground beef

1 small onion, chopped

1 can whole corn, drained

1 small can sliced olives

1 can red kidney beans, drained

1 can stewed tomatoes

1 tablespoon chili powder or chipotle spice blend

Salt & pepper to taste

DAY OF -

2 cups Fritos

To Prepare:

Cook the beef and onion until done. Let cool and place in freezer bag with all the other ingredients except the Fritos. Let air out and seal. Freeze until ready to use.

To Cook:

Defrost in fridge overnight.

SLOW COOKER - Place bag contents in slow cooker and cook on low for 2 to 4 hours. Just before serving, top with the chips.

PRESSURE COOKER - Place bag contents in pressure cooker. Cook on high for 3 minutes. QR

Luau Pork (Kahlua Pig)

INGREDIENTS:

1 4 to 5 pound pork butt roast or pork shoulder roast
3 tablespoons liquid smoke flavoring
1 tablespoon crushed garlic

DAY OF -
Banana leaves (optional)

To Prepare:

Pierce pork all over with a carving fork or knife. Place in bag. Add liquid smoke. Rub into meat well.

This needs to marinate for a few days in the freezer. Be sure to let it defrost for about 10 hours in your fridge before cooking.

To Cook: This recipe turns out *best* in a slow cooker.

SLOW COOKER - Put ¼ cup of water in the bottom of the slow cooker. Line slow cooker with banana leaves (optional). Place contents of bag in slow cooker and wrap leaves around roast. Cover, and cook on low for at least 10 to 20 hours, turning a couple of times during cooking. Add another 1/4 cup water if needed.

Remove meat from slow cooker. Discard banana leaves and shred the meat, adding drippings as needed to moisten.

PRESSURE COOKER - Put 1 cup of water in the bottom of the slow cooker. Place contents of bag in pressure cooker. Cover, and cook on high for 16 minutes. NR for 4 minutes then QR.

To Serve:

Pop about two or three cups of shredded cabbage in the slow cooker for the last hour or so or in a pressure cooker for 2 minutes (once back up to pressure). This is how it's served in Hawaii. You can eat in sweet Hawaiian bread rolls, or just on the plate. Authentic with rice and macaroni salad.

Orange Shrimp

INGREDIENTS:

1 pound fresh or frozen cooked shrimp, cleaned
1 bag frozen broccoli
1 tablespoon orange zest
1/4 cup orange juice
1/4 cup olive oil
2 tablespoons crushed garlic
1/2 cup shredded carrots
1/4 teaspoon crushed red pepper flakes

To Prepare:

Place all items in freezer bag. Let air out and seal. Freeze until ready to use.

To Cook:

Defrost bag in fridge before cooking.

SLOW COOKER -   Place bag contents in slow cooker and cook on low for 2 to 3 hours.

PRESSURE COOKER -   Place bag contents in pressure cooker and cook on high for 2 to 3 minutes.

To Serve:

Serve over rice with a crunchy slaw!

Menu #3 Meal Grocery Lists

Mongolian Beef
1-1/2 pounds flank steak, cut into strips
2 tablespoons olive oil
1 teaspoon grated fresh ginger
3/4 cup soy sauce
3/4 cup water
3/4 cup honey
1 cup shredded carrots
1/2 brown onion, chopped
Juice of one lemon
2 tablespoons minced garlic

Sri Lankan Coconut Chicken
4 boneless chicken breasts
1 can coconut milk or cream (not water)
1 teaspoon crushed garlic
¼ onion, minced
1 teaspoon ground turmeric
1 teaspoon fresh fennel, minced or 1 teaspoon fennel seed, crushed
1 tablespoon fresh ginger, grated
Black pepper to taste
Juice from 1 lime
A pinch of chili flakes (if desired)
Salt to taste
½ teaspoon cinnamon
1/2 cup shredded (unsweetened) coconut

Luau Pork
1 4 to 5 pound pork butt roast or pork shoulder roast
3 tablespoons liquid smoke flavoring
Banana leaves (optional)

Salsa Beef
1.5 pounds beef stew meat
2 cups salsa
1 tablespoon crushed garlic
2 tablespoons lemon juice

Creamy Italian Chicken
4 chicken breasts, cut into strips if desired
8 ounce package of cream cheese
1 can of cream of chicken soup
1 small bottle of Italian dressing
1 teaspoon Italian seasoning

Cowboy Casserole
1 pound ground beef
1 small onion, chopped
1 can whole corn, drained
1 small can sliced olives
1 can red kidney beans, drained
1 can stewed tomatoes
chili powder
chipotle spice blend
salt & pepper to taste

Orange Shrimp
1 pound fresh or frozen cooked shrimp, cleaned
1 bag frozen broccoli
1 tablespoon shredded orange peel
1/4 cup orange juice
1/4 cup olive oil
2 tablespoons crushed garlic
1/2 cup shredded carrots
1/4 teaspoon crushed red pepper flakes

Menu #4

Korean Beef (Bulgogi)
Tomato Parmesan Roast
Orange Chicken
Chicken Ole'

Meatloaf
Thai Peanut Pork
Lemon Dill Tilapia

Menu #4 Grocery List

Meats
2 to 3 pound sirloin tip roast, thinly sliced
2 pound chuck roast
4 boneless, skinless chicken breasts
4 servings of boneless, skinless chicken pieces
1-1/2 pounds lean ground beef
4 large boneless pork chops
4 servings of fresh tilapia fillets

Produce
1 bunch green onions
2 lemons
2 red bell peppers
5 tablespoons fresh ginger
1 small onion

Packaged
1 can corn
1 can black beans
1/2 cup chunky peanut butter
4 tablespoons brown sugar
8 Tablespoons sugar
2 Tablespoon flour
2 cups salsa

1 cup chicken broth
1 cup grated Parmesan cheese
½ cup sun-dried tomatoes
3 tablespoon honey
4 tablespoons sesame oil
2 teaspoons olive oil
1 tablespoon Worcestershire sauce
about 1 cup soy sauce
2 pieces sliced bread (any kind)
1/2 cup bread crumbs
4 tablespoons sesame seeds
6 tablespoons crushed garlic

Dairy
1 cup milk
1 egg

Spices
Onion powder
Paprika
Dill
Red chili flakes
Fresh rosemary
Salt & pepper

Things to Prep for Menu #4

Slice green onions thinly

Cut chicken breasts into large cubes

Cut pork chops into bite-size pieces

Slice roast thinly

Bulgogi Beef (Korean Beef)

INGREDIENTS:

2 to 3 pound sirloin tip roast, thinly sliced

8 Tablespoons sugar

4 Tablespoons sesame oil

8 Tablespoons soy sauce

1 bunch green onions, sliced

4 cloves of garlic, crushed

2 Tablespoons Lemon juice

4 Tablespoons sesame seeds

2 Tablespoon flour

DAY OF -

1/2 cup water

To Prepare:

Combine all ingredients, except water in a freezer bag. Gently knead the marinade with the beef.

To Cook:

Defrost bag in fridge before cooking.

SLOW COOKER:

Place contents of bag in slow cooker. Put 1/2 cup water into bag to swish out sauce contents and put in slow cooker. Cook on high for 4 hours or on low for 8 hours.

PRESSURE COOKER: Place contents of bag in pressure cooker. Put 1/2 cup water into bag to swish out sauce contents and put in pressure cooker. Cook on high for 20 minutes. QR

To Serve:

Top with additional sliced green onions and more sesame seeds. Goes well with rice and any veggie or salad.

Tomato Parmesan Pot Roast

INGREDIENTS:

2 pound chuck roast

1½ teaspoons salt

½ teaspoon pepper

1 cup grated Parmesan cheese

½ cup finely chopped sun-dried tomatoes

2 teaspoons fresh rosemary, finely chopped

2 tablespoons minced garlic

To Prepare:

Place all items in freezer bag except roast. Mix well. Add roast and press other ingredients into meat to create a crust. Let air out and seal. Freeze until ready to use.

To Cook:

Defrost in fridge overnight.

SLOW COOKER: Place bag contents in slow cooker. Cover and cook on high for 4 hours or 8 hours on low. Turn off slow cooker and remove from base if possible. Remove lid and allow roast to rest for 10 to 15 minutes before slicing.

PRESSURE COOKER: Place bag contents in slow cooker. Add 1 cup water or beef broth and cook on high for 22 minutes. NR for 5 minutes then QR. Allow roast to rest for 10 to 15 minutes before slicing.

Orange Chicken

INGREDIENTS:

4 boneless chicken breasts
1 cup bar-b-q sauce (Sweet Baby Rays suggested)
1 cup orange marmalade
2 tablespoons soy sauce
Zest of an orange
1/2 to 1 teaspoon red pepper flakes

To Prepare:

Cut chicken into large cubes. Combine everything in a freezer bag. Mix well. Seal bag and freeze until ready for use.

To Cook:

Thaw overnight in refrigerator before cooking.

This meal is *best* when baked in the oven.

OVEN:

Place mixture in baking dish. Cover with foil. Bake at 350° for 35 minutes. Remove foil and bake for an additional 25 minutes.

SLOW COOKER: Place mixture in slow cooker and cook on low for 3 to 4 hours or until cooked through and tender.

PRESSURE COOKER: Place mixture in pressure cooker and cook on high for 6 minutes.

To Serve:

Serve over rice.

Chicken Ole'

INGREDIENTS:

4 servings of boneless, skinless chicken pieces
1 can corn, drained
1 can black beans, drained
2 cups salsa
1 teaspoon onion powder
1 teaspoon paprika

To Prepare:

Place all items in freezer bag and mix well. Let air out and seal. Freeze until ready to use.

To Cook:

Defrost bag in fridge before cooking.

SLOW COOKER: Place bag contents in slow cooker and cook on low for 6 to 8 hours. Shred chicken and stir back into sauce.

PRESSURE COOKER: Place bag contents in pressure cooker and cook on high for 7 minutes. Shred chicken and stir back into sauce.

To Serve:

Serve over rice or in tortillas.

Basic Meatloaf

1 1/2 pounds lean ground beef
1/2 cup bread crumbs
1 cup milk
1 tablespoon Worcestershire sauce
1/2 teaspoon salt & pepper
1 egg
1 small onion, finely diced
2 pieces sliced bread (any kind)

Suggested Add Ins

- Add 2 teaspoons Italian seasoning to mix. Cover with spaghetti sauce 10 minutes before removing from oven.
- Use half pork sausage instead of just ground beef.
- Cut the loaf in half lengthwise. Put shredded or chunk cheese in the center and reform top of loaf onto bottom. Cover top with ketchup 10 minutes before removing from oven.
- Use different spices in the mix like Cajun or rosemary.
- Cover with tomato sauce 10 minutes before removing from oven.
- Take out the Worcestershire sauce and put in 4 tablespoons of bar-b-q sauce.
- Make loaf with ground pork. Add 3 tablespoons fresh ground ginger. Take out the Worcestershire sauce and add 2 tablespoons soy sauce. Cover with teriyaki sauce 10 minutes before removing from oven.
- Add 1/3 cup ketchup to mix and then pour another 1/2 cup on top.

To Prepare:

Mix all ingredients except bread together. Add in any other ingredients you want (see suggestions above). Form into a loaf. Place bread in foil pan or baking dish then put meatloaf on top. Wrap well with plastic wrap then foil. Freeze until ready to use. (The bread soaks up the fat from the meat.)

To Cook:

Thaw overnight in refrigerator before cooking. Preheat oven to 350°. Bake uncovered at 350° for about an hour. Let cool and serve.

To Serve:

Always good with mashed potatoes!

Thai Peanut Pork

INGREDIENTS:

4 large boneless pork chops
2 red bell peppers
1/3 cup soy sauce
1/2 cup chunky peanut butter
1 tablespoon fresh ginger, grated

1 cup chicken broth
3 tablespoon honey
1 teaspoon crushed garlic
1 teaspoon red pepper flakes

DAY OF -

Crushed peanuts if desired

To Prepare:

Cut pork into bite sized pieces Cut peppers into strips. Put all ingredients into freezer bag and mix. Let air out of bag and freeze until ready to use.

To Cook:

Defrost bag in fridge before cooking.

SLOW COOKER: Put bag contents into slow cooker. Cook on low for 4 to 5 hours or on high for 3 hours or until pork is tender and has reached 165 degrees.

PRESSURE COOKER: Put bag contents into pressure cooker. Cook on high for 5 minutes. NR for 5 minutes then QR.

To Serve:

Top with crispy Asian noodles or crushed peanuts. Great over noodles or rice and most any veggie or salad.

Lemon Dill Tilapia

INGREDIENTS:

4 to 6 fresh tilapia fillets

2 teaspoons olive oil

Juice and zest from 1 lemon

1 tablespoon dill

1 teaspoon crushed garlic

To Prepare:

Mix all ingredients except fish in freezer bag. Add fish. Remove air, seal and freeze until ready for use.

To Cook:

Defrost bag in fridge before cooking. Heat grill to medium-high heat. Cook tilapia for 5 to 7 minutes or until fish is opaque.

You can also bake in your oven at 375° for 20 minutes.

To Serve: Serve with any veggie or salad. You can also put in corn tortillas and serve as fish tacos.

Menu #4 Meal Grocery Lists

Bulgogi Beef

2 to 3 pound sirloin tip roast, thinly sliced
8 Tablespoons sugar
4 Tablespoons sesame oil
8 Tablespoons soy sauce
1 bunch green onions, sliced
4 cloves of garlic, crushed
2 Tablespoons Lemon juice
4 Tablespoons sesame seeds
2 Tablespoon flour

Orange Chicken

4 boneless chicken breasts
1 cup bar-b-q sauce (Sweet Baby Rays suggested)

1 cup orange marmalade

2 tablespoons soy sauce

Zest of an orange

1/2 to 1 teaspoon red pepper flakes

Thai Peanut Pork

4 large boneless pork chops
2 red bell peppers
1/3 cup soy sauce
1/2 cup chunky peanut butter
1 tablespoon fresh ginger, grated
1 cup chicken broth
3 tablespoon honey
1 teaspoon crushed garlic
1 teaspoon red pepper flakes

Tomato Parmesan Roast

2 pound chuck roast
1½ teaspoons salt
½ teaspoon pepper
1 cup grated Parmesan cheese
½ cup finely chopped sun-dried tomatoes
2 teaspoons fresh rosemary, finely chopped
2 tablespoons minced garlic

Chicken Ole'

4 servings of boneless, skinless chicken pieces
1 can corn, drained
1 can black beans, drained
2 cups salsa
1 teaspoon onion powder
1 teaspoon paprika

Meatloaf

1-1/2 pounds lean ground beef
1/2 cup bread crumbs
1 cup milk
1 tablespoon Worcestershire sauce
1/2 teaspoon salt & pepper
1 egg
1 small onion, finely diced
2 pieces sliced bread (any kind)
Additional spices or sauces

Lemon Dill Tilapia

4 to 6 fresh tilapia fillets
2 teaspoons olive oil
Juice and zest from 1 lemon
1 tablespoon dill
1 teaspoon crushed garlic

Menu #5

Round Steak
Indonesian Beef Rending
Garlic Ranch Chicken
Butter Chicken

Chili & Beans
Raspberry Chipotle Pork Roast
Honey Garlic Shrimp

Menu #5 Grocery List

Meats
1-1/2 pounds beef top round steak
2 pounds beef rump roast
4 boneless skinless chicken breasts
2 pounds boneless skinless chicken thighs
2 pounds lean ground beef
1 pork roast (2-3 pounds)
1 pound large shrimp, peeled and deveined

Produce
4 large potatoes
4 onions
1 piece of fresh ginger
1 medium red bell pepper
4 red chilies
2 lemons
2 tablespoons lemongrass stalks,

Packaged
1 10 ounce can cream of mushroom soup
1 10 ounce can cream of chicken soup
1 envelope onion soup mix
1 packet dry ranch dressing mix
1 (8 ounce) can tomato paste
1 (8 ounce) can tomato sauce
1 (14-ounce) can tomato sauce

1 (28-ounce) can diced tomatoes
2 (15-ounce) cans kidney beans
2 14 or 15 ounce cans coconut milk
1/4 cup coarsely chopped pickled jalapeños or green chilies (optional)
½ cup honey
¼ cup soy sauce
2 tablespoons sugar
3 tablespoons tamarind paste
1 cup raspberry syrup jam
about 12 tablespoons crushed garlic

Dairy
4 tablespoons butter

Spices
Cajun spice
Chipotle Seasoning
Chili powder
cinnamon
Coriander
Cumin
Curry powder
Garam Masala
Paprika
Turmeric

Things to Prep for Menu #5

Peel and cube potatoes

Chop 1 onion

Chop chilies

Chop jalapenos

Chop lemongrass

Cut chicken thighs into bite-size pieces

Brown ground beef with 2 diced onions

Stick to Your Ribs Round Steak

INGREDIENTS:

4 large potatoes, peeled and cubed

1-1/2 pounds beef top round steak

1 can cream of mushroom soup

½ cup water

1 envelope onion soup mix

1 tablespoon crushed garlic

Pepper to taste

To Prepare:

Place all items in freezer bag. Mix well. Let air out and seal. Freeze until ready to use.

To Cook:

Defrost in fridge overnight.

SLOW COOKER: Place bag contents in slow cooker. Cook on low for 6 to 8 hours.

PRESSURE COOKER: Place bag contents in pressure cooker. Cook on high for 20 minutes.

Indonesian Beef Rendang

INGREDIENTS:

2 pounds beef rump roast or other braising beef
1 large onion, chopped
4 tablespoons crushed garlic
2 tablespoons grated fresh ginger
4 red chilies, chopped
2 tablespoons sugar
2 teaspoons coriander

2 tablespoons lemon juice
3 tablespoons tamarind paste
1 teaspoon ground turmeric
1 teaspoon cumin
2 tablespoons lemongrass stalks, finely chopped
1 14 oz. can coconut milk
Pinch of salt

To Prepare:

Trim all fat and cut the beef into 2" pieces.

Place onion, garlic, ginger, chilies, sugar, coriander, lemon juice, tamarind, turmeric, cumin, salt and chopped lemongrass into a freezer bag. Pound bag until the mixture is a paste. Add coconut milk and mix again. Add beef and mix well. Let the air out and seal. Freeze until ready to use.

To Cook:

Defrost in fridge overnight.

SLOW COOKER: Place bag contents in slow cooker. Cook on low 4 to 6 hours; there will be quite a bit of liquid in the pot. Stir, and then turn the slow cooker to high and set the lid slightly off. Continue to cook for 2 to 3 hours on high until the excess liquid has evaporated. Serve over cooked rice.

PRESSURE COOKER: Place bag contents in pressure cooker. Cook on high for 20 minutes. QR. If there is too much liquid, turn on simmer for a few minutes while stirring.

Garlic Ranch Chicken

INGREDIENTS:

4 boneless skinless chicken breasts

1 10 ounce can cream of chicken soup

2 tablespoons crushed garlic

1 packet dry ranch dressing mix

To Prepare:

If you like, you can cube the chicken or use the breasts whole. Put all ingredients into freezer bag. Mix together and freeze until ready to use.

To Cook:

Defrost bag in fridge before cooking.

SLOW COOKER: Put bag contents into slow cooker. Cook on low for 5 to 6 hours or on high for 3 to 4 hours or until chicken is tender and has reached 165 degrees.

PRESSURE COOKER: Put bag contents into pressure cooker. Cook on high for 6 minutes. QR.

To Serve:

Great with roasted potatoes, noodles or rice and most any veggie or salad.

Butter Chicken

INGREDIENTS:

2 pounds boneless skinless chicken thighs
1 8 ounce can tomato paste
1 8 ounce can tomato sauce
1 15 ounce can coconut milk
1 tablespoon minced ginger
3 teaspoons minced garlic

1/2 onion, finely minced
2 teaspoons Garam Masala
1 teaspoon curry powder
1/2 teaspoon cinnamon
1 teaspoon salt
1 teaspoon pepper
3 tablespoons butter

DAY OF –

½ cup plain Greek yogurt

More butter

To Prepare:

Cut chicken into bite sized pieces. Mince the onion (I actually grate it so it's very fine). Combine all ingredients except chicken in freezer bag. Mix well. Add chicken and mix again. Seal bag and freeze until ready for use.

To Cook:

Thaw overnight in refrigerator before cooking.

SLOW COOKER - Place mixture in slow cooker. Cook on low for 8 hours. Before serving add yogurt and more butter (just a couple of pats). Mix well.

PRESSURE COOKER - Place mixture in pressure cooker. Cook on high for 6 minutes. Before serving add yogurt and more butter (just a couple of pats). Mix well.

To Serve:

Serve with cooked brown rice and green veggies.

Chili & Beans

INGREDIENTS:

2 pounds lean ground beef

2 medium yellow onions, diced

1 medium red bell pepper, diced

4 teaspoons crushed garlic

2 tablespoons chili powder

1 tablespoon paprika

1 teaspoon chipotle or Cajun spice

1 (28-ounce) can diced tomatoes (do not drain)

1 (14-ounce) can tomato sauce

2 (15-ounce) cans kidney beans (drained)

1/4 cup coarsely chopped pickled jalapeños or green chilies, drained (optional)

To Prepare:

Brown the meat and onion together. Let cool and place in freezer bag with all other ingredients. Let air out and seal. Freeze until ready to use.

To Cook:

Defrost in fridge overnight.

SLOW COOKER - Place bag contents in slow cooker. Cook about 6 hours on low or 4 hours on high.

PRESSURE COOKER - Place bag contents in pressure cooker. Cook on high for 8 minutes. NR for 5 minutes then QR.

To Serve:

Serve topped with the cheese, scallions, and sour cream.

Raspberry Chipotle Pork Roast

INGREDIENTS:

1 pork roast (2-3 pounds)
2 Tablespoons Chipotle Seasoning
1 cup raspberry syrup   ~**or**~ 1 cup raspberry jam

To Prepare:

Put roast in freezer bag and rub with chipotle. Poor syrup or jam over the top and mix.

To Cook:

Thaw overnight in refrigerator before cooking.

SLOW COOKER: Cook in slow cooker for 6 to 8 hours on low.

PRESSURE COOKER: Cook in pressure on high for 15 minutes. QR.

OVEN: You can also bake this in your oven. Bake, uncovered, at 350° for 1-3/4 to 2 hours or until a meat thermometer reads 160°.

Let stand for 10 to 15 minutes before slicing.

To Serve:

Yummy with most any veggie or salad and potatoes.

Honey Garlic Shrimp

INGREDIENTS:

½ cup honey
¼ cup soy sauce
2 tablespoons crushed garlic
juice of one small lemon
1 pound large shrimp, peeled and deveined
1 tablespoons butter
Salt & pepper to taste

DAY OF -

Green onions, for garnish

To Prepare:

Place all ingredients into freezer bag and mix. Seal bag and freeze until ready to use.

To Cook:

Thaw overnight in refrigerator before cooking.

Place bag contents into a medium sized skillet. Turn the heat to medium high. Cook until the shrimp turns pink about 2 minutes each side. pour the marinade over shrimp. Cook until the sauce starts to thicken and coats the shrimp. Garnish with green onions.

Menu #5 Meal Grocery Lists

Round Steak
4 large potatoes, peeled and cubed
1.5 pounds beef top round steak
1 can cream of mushroom soup
½ cup water
1 envelope onion soup mix
1 tablespoon crushed garlic
Pepper to taste

Chili & Beans
2 pounds lean ground beef
2 medium yellow onions, diced
1 medium red bell pepper, diced
4 teaspoons crushed garlic
2 tablespoons chili powder
1 tablespoon paprika
1 teaspoon chipotle or Cajun spice
1 (28-ounce) can diced tomatoes (do not drain)
1 (14-ounce) can tomato sauce
2 (15-ounce) cans kidney beans (drained)
1/4 cup coarsely chopped pickled jalapeños or green chilies, drained (optional)

Indonesian Beef Rending
2 pounds beef rump roast or other braising beef
1 large onion, chopped
4 tablespoons crushed garlic
2 tablespoons grated fresh ginger
4 red chilies, chopped
2 tablespoons sugar
2 teaspoons coriander
2 tablespoons lemon juice
3 tablespoons tamarind paste
1 teaspoon ground turmeric
1 teaspoon cumin
2 tablespoons lemongrass stalks, finely chopped
1 14 oz. can coconut milk
Pinch of salt

Butter Chicken
2 pounds boneless skinless chicken thighs
1 8 ounce can tomato paste
1 8 ounce can tomato sauce
1 15 ounce can coconut milk
1 tablespoon minced ginger
3 teaspoons minced garlic
1/2 onion, finely minced
2 teaspoons Garam Masala
1 teaspoon curry powder
1/2 teaspoon cinnamon
1 teaspoon salt
1 teaspoon pepper
3 tablespoons butter

Honey Garlic Shrimp
½ cup honey
¼ cup soy sauce
2 tablespoons crushed garlic
juice of one small lemon
1 pound large shrimp, peeled and deveined
1 tablespoons butter
Salt & pepper to taste

Garlic Ranch Chicken
4 boneless skinless chicken breasts
1 10 ounce can cream of chicken soup
2 tablespoons crushed garlic
1 packet dry ranch dressing mix

Raspberry Chipotle Pork Roast
1 pork roast (2-3 pounds)
2 Tablespoons Chipotle Seasoning
1 cup raspberry syrup ~or~ raspberry jam

Grocery List For All 5 Weeks

Meats
2 pounds beef rump roast or other braising beef
2 to 3 pound sirloin tip roast, thinly sliced
2 pound chuck roast
2 pound boneless beef chuck shoulder roast
1.5 pounds beef stew meat
1-1/2 pounds beef top round steak
5-1/2 pounds of flank steak
2 to 3 pounds beef ribs
2 pounds boneless skinless chicken thighs
4 servings of chicken pieces
32 boneless skinless chicken breasts
8 large boneless pork chops
2 pound boneless pork loin
1 pork roast (2-3 pounds)
A 4 pound pork butt roast
5-1/2 pounds lean ground beef
4 servings of fresh tilapia fillets
4 fresh tuna, salmon or swordfish filets
2 pounds large shrimp, peeled and deveined

Produce
12 to 15 medium potatoes
1-1/2 cups shredded carrots
5 carrots
3 red bell peppers
1 stalk of celery
11 onions
1 red onion
1 bunch green onions
1 jalapeno
4 red chilies
1 cup fresh cilantro
2 tablespoons lemongrass stalks
1 cup fresh mushrooms
1 pound broccoli florets
1 apple
6 lemons
2 oranges
3 limes
enough fresh ginger for 12 tablespoons grated

Packaged
4 (15-ounce) cans kidney beans
2 cans black beans
1 small can sliced olives
3 cans whole corn
1 can of whole berry cranberry sauce
1 can stewed tomatoes
2 (28-ounce) cans diced tomatoes
1 (8 ounce) can tomato paste
1 (8 ounce) can tomato sauce
1 (14-ounce) can tomato sauce
2 10 ounce cans cream of mushroom soup
4 cans cream of chicken soup
26 ounces beef broth
1 cup chicken broth
2 packets of dry onion soup mix
1 small bottle of Italian dressing
8 ounce bottle of French dressing
3 packages dry Ranch Dressing mix
1/4 cup pickled jalapeños or green chilies (optional)
4 cups salsa
½ cup sun-dried tomatoes
3 cups +3 tablespoons honey
2 cups raspberry syrup or preserves
1/2 cup chunky peanut butter
3 tablespoons rice vinegar
1/2 cup balsamic vinegar
4 cans coconut milk or cream (not water)
about 32 tablespoons crushed garlic
10 tablespoons sugar
about 1 cup brown sugar
3 tablespoons tamarind paste
9 tablespoons sesame oil
About 2 cups olive oil
3 tablespoons liquid smoke flavoring
1 cup ketchup
1 small bottle bar-b-q sauce
about 3/4 cup Worcestershire sauce
About 4-1/2 cups soy sauce
1 teaspoon cornstarch
2 Tablespoon flour

1/2 cup bread crumbs
1 cup grated Parmesan cheese
8 tablespoons sesame seeds
1/2 cup shredded (unsweetened) coconut
3-3/4 cups orange juice
¾ cups apple juice
3 tablespoons lemon juice
2 pieces sliced bread (any kind)

Frozen
1 pound fresh or frozen cooked shrimp, cleaned
1 bag frozen broccoli
1 cup pitted cherries
1 (28 ounce) bag frozen meatballs
16 ounce bag frozen peach slices

Dairy
4 tablespoons butter
2 cups milk
1 egg
8 ounce package of cream cheese

Spices
Cajun spice
Chili powder
Chipotle seasoning
Cinnamon
Coriander
Crushed red pepper flakes
Cumin
Curry powder
Dill
Fresh fennel, minced or fennel seed, crushed
Fresh rosemary
Garam Masala
Ground coriander
Ground turmeric
Italian seasoning
Onion powder
Onion powder
Paprika
Salt & pepper
Turmeric

Things to Prep for All 35 Meals

Veggies -

Cut 2 onions into wedges

Chop 4 onions (3 to be cooked with ground beef)

Cut carrots into bite size pieces

Slice red onion

Chop mushrooms

Peel and cube potatoes

Cut potatoes into large pieces

Slice green onions thinly

Chop chilies

Chop jalapenos

Chop lemongrass

Meats -

Cut 2 pounds of steak into thin slices

Cut ribs apart, if needed

Cook ground beef with 1 chopped onion

Brown ground beef with 2 diced onions

Cook ground beef and cool

Leave 1 pound of ground beef uncooked

Cut pork chops into bite-size pieces

Slice sirloin roast thinly

Cut 12 chicken breasts in half lengthwise (like strips)

Cut 4 chicken breasts into strips

Cut chicken breasts into large cubes

Cut chicken thighs into bite-size pieces

Recipe Index

Apple Cherry Pork Loin - - - - - - - - - - - - - - - - - - 30

Balsamic Beef Roast with Carrots - - - - - - - - - - - 16

BBQ Beef Ribs - 27

Beef & Broccoli - 26

Butter Chicken - 59

Carne Asada - 17

Chicken Ole' - 49

Chili & Beans - 60

Cowboy Casserole - - - - - - - - - - - - - - - - - - - 40

Creamy Italian Chicken - - - - - - - - - - - - - - - - 39

French Chicken - 29

Garlic Ranch Chicken - - - - - - - - - - - - - - - - - 58

Ginger Peach Chicken - - - - - - - - - - - - - - - - - 19

Honey Garlic Shrimp - - - - - - - - - - - - - - - - - 62

Honey Sesame Chicken - - - - - - - - - - - - - - - - 28

Indonesian Beef Rending - - - - - - - - - - - - - - - 57

Korean Beef (Bulgogi) - - - - - - - - - - - - - - - - - 46

Lemon Dill Tilapia - - - - - - - - - - - - - - - - - - - 52

Luau Pork (Kalua Pig) - - - - - - - - - - - - - - - - - 41

Marinated Fish - 32

Meatloaf - 50

Mongolian Beef	36
Orange Chicken	48
Orange Shrimp	42
Ranch Pork Chops	21
Raspberry Chipotle Chicken	18
Raspberry Chipotle Pork Roast	61
Round Steak	56
Salsa Beef	37
Sri Lankan Coconut Chicken	38
Swedish Meatballs	20
Taco Soup	30
Teriyaki Shrimp	22
Thai Peanut Pork	51
Tomato Parmesan Roast	47

ABOUT THE AUTHOR

When I was working full time I would put together a bunch of meals for the freezer every other Sunday.

I have been doing freezer meal **workshops** since 2010. I do them for people who want to host in their homes and for various city recreation programs.

I'm always looking for and creating new recipes.

Check out my website if you're interested in hosting or attending a workshop.
http://freezerworkshop.angelfire.com

If you're interested in doing Freezer Meal Workshops to earn some extra money, check out my book -
How to do Freezer Meal Workshops for Fun & Profit
At www.annieshousepublishing.com

If you'd like to order another copy of this book for a friend or to order upcoming volumes go to
www.annieshousepublishing.com

Made in the USA
Middletown, DE
07 October 2022